JUNKIE WIFE

JUNKIE WIFE

poems by
Alexis Rhone Fancher

MOON
TIDE PRESS

~ 2018 ~

Editor-in-chief
Eric Morago

Associate Editor
Michael Miller

Marketing Specialist
Caitlin Hawekotte

Proofreader
Jim Hoggatt

Front cover photo of the author
Jerry Vaughn

Book design
Michael Wada

Moon Tide logo design
Abraham Gomez

Junkie Wife
is published by Moon Tide Press

Moon Tide Press #166
6745 Washington Ave.
Whittier, CA 90601
www.moontidepress.com

FIRST EDITION

Printed in the United States of America

ISBN #978-0-9974837-4-1

FURTHER PRAISE FOR JUNKIE WIFE...

Nothing shocks this poet with her sharp photographer's eye, her sustained attention on the grit and addiction and sex against the neon of Hollywood Blvd. And yet each admission, each detail so carefully wrought in its rawness and pain—a punch to the gut. Rhone Fancher's wit and candor born of survival are apparent in every line, the tongue-in-cheek and wink of every poem a delight to follow, as in "Coercion" after Margaret Atwood, in which the speaker plays with tradition in the brassy voice of *The Junkie Wife*: "Back then, we fit together like / cooking spoons in a drawer. // Bent spoons. A cadaver drawer." This poet recognizes the grime beneath the shimmer. She never looks away.

— Jennifer Givhan, author of *Landscape with Headless Mama*

Alexis Rhone Fancher writes with the intensity of one who's been there, lived the life, survived it, then went back for seconds. 'Raw' and 'bold' are words that come to mind from the start, but those are prurient, rubbernecking words for the sex-and-drugs lifestyle Fancher describes with precision. Better words are those from AA/NA 12-step programs: 'brutal honesty.' The poet holds a magnifying glass to the glitzy illusions so her readers can see cracks where dark seeps in. She then exploits that ugliness for its beauty in the same way one who is both junkie and wife/lover might be exploited for hers. "Him on me," she writes, "a miasma of scorching discontent." The juxtapositions between love and contempt, nostalgia and regret, make *Junkie Wife* one of the most compelling collections of poetry I've read. Like any addict, I want more and more. Fancher delivers one line at a time.

— Ace Boggess, author of *Ultra Deep Field* and *The Prisoners*

Alexis Rhone Fancher doesn't flirt. Her poems are all energy; the images and narratives she chooses create a dynamic landscape. In "Junkie Wife," her talents are on full display. The poems in this playful, sexy chapbook are fierce, thick flicks of her poetic capability, the kind of poetry you don't often get to experience.

— Darren C. Demaree, author of *Two Towns Over*

for Fancher

CONTENTS

FOREWORD

"HE THOUGHT IT MEANT I LOVED HIM" – *JUNKIE WIFE* AND THE ADDICTION THAT'S BETTER THAN SEX

Sam Fuller once observed that "Life is in color, but black and white is more real." In striving to record the injectable life behind the colors of bodily cravings, Alexis Rhone Fancher has chosen the equivalent of black and white film to imprint the poems of her latest assemblage, *Junkie Wife*. While the flamboyant titular modifier still retains the allure of smoldering, forbidden degradation, the more pedestrian noun, in fact, ends up propelling the narrative, for at the penetralia of Fancher's often harrowing images of addiction, one finds the warped marriage vows that every junkie recites: "I need this more than it needs me, but still it gives itself wholly to my needs."

The subject matter of this chapbook will hardly be unfamiliar territory to experienced readers. Indeed, the quotation of Sam Fuller was borrowed from its use as an epigraph in a poem by the late, great Linda Hull, whose work should probably be a required encounter prior to reading *Junkie Wife*; and though other readers might regard some of the poems of Kate Ellen Braverman or Kim Addonizio's *Jimmy and Rita* as the poetic soul mates of Alexis Rhone Fancher's *Junkie Wife*, I detect a more distant counterpart than other renowned work in this domain such as Nelson Algren's *The Man with the Golden Arm*. Years ago, reading several novels by Zola and Flaubert back to back, I could not help but notice the grim fates of their women characters. The title character of *Nana* ends up dying gruesomely, as is the fate of the alcoholic wife in *L'Assomoir*. Ditto *Madame Bovary*. Fancher will have none of this patriarchal condescension in which women are dutifully punished for being outlaws. The penultimate poem in *Junkie Wife*, for instance, offers the cautionary signal of "I can see my future, / and I'm not in it." In making the distinction between "my future" and "the future," the escape tunnel from the prisoner-of-drugs camp must seem only slightly larger than a syringe. Somehow, though, it must be burrowed through to attain liberation from the bondage of being no more capable of seeing her future than comprehending the almost total eclipse of her past.

Fortunately, Fancher's skill in delineating the essential images includes her deft alternation of verb tense. As she walks (present tense) the streets of Hollywood, her face is no doubt having "marks of weakness, marks of woe" encroach upon it, if only out of wincing empathy for the youthful harlot being toyed with by "two men the size of refrigerators." Technique is all too easy to overlook in free verse that inhabits a *noir* mise-en-scene, but let us note how Fancher's control of tempo derives from her fine use of end-stopped lines, which normally hamper a free-verse poem, to tamper down any melodramatic aura that the reader might bring to the subject matter or her themes.

Two of this collection's most memorable poems are the first one, "Flirting with Death," and "The Dracaena Plant in my Apartment on Beachwood Dr." The latter reminds me somewhat of Charles Bukowski's "The Tragedy of the Leaves," which is frequently anthologized. Fancher's poem equally deserves that kind of encore. Indeed, memorable images twist and turn throughout these poems, though the afterglow of each image differs in how it manipulates our memory of what we just read and its consequences: are we, too, as readers succumbing to the insatiable desire for the perverse "rush" of voyeuristic fulfillment? Hard not to, when the poet is so forthcoming about the protagonist's complicity. That poem ends with a touch of almost comic irony, which I will not quote but let you savor as your special reward.

Although Fuller is known for his noir films, my favorite scene in one of Sam Fuller's most searing films, *The Big Red One*, shows a group of soldiers sitting around and waiting for the next onslaught of murderous chaos to commence. A new, very young soldier has shown up, and is chattering nervously, wondering about his chances of surviving the war. Seeking reassurance that the odds might slightly favor him, the replacement pleads for succor, "You don't think I'll get killed, do you?" "Why not?" replies one of the veterans. "You somebody special?"

In journeying through the caustic self-dissolution of addiction, Fancher makes certain that she strips the reader of any illusion that she regards herself as "special." "Spiritual combat is as harrowing as physical combat," Rimbaud says in *Une Saison en Enfer*, a thought that should be even better known than his self-extrapolation of "J'est un autre." In *Junkie Wife*, Alexis Rhone Fancher has returned from the front lines and we should be grateful for her candor.

Bill Mohr
February 10, 2018

Bill Mohr is the author of *Holdouts: The Los Angeles Poetry Renaissance 1948-1992* (University of Iowa Press, 2011) as well as several volumes of poems. He is a professor of English at CSU Long Beach.

No names were changed.
No one was innocent.

FLIRTING WITH DEATH - A LOVE POEM

1.
In love with the rush. Not the high.
I'd shoot up again and again.
He was a born rescuer.
I was perfect, a bottomless pit.

We sniffed around each other like dogs.
"It takes one to know one," he said.

2.
Before we went to bed
we went to dinner.
He kept hold of my right hand.
"I'm afraid of overdosing," I confessed
over coffee.

His voice had a nasal quality.
"Marry me," he begged.

3.
In the beginning, we were fierce lovers.

4.
"Shoot me up," he'd plead, toward the end.
But I wouldn't.
He thought it meant I loved him.

5.
I didn't.
I wanted the drugs for myself.

THINGS I PUT IN MY MOUTH

repressed desire
a gin martini
a one-night stand

a hangnail
kung pao chicken
a sleepless night

your first edition of *Being & Nothingness*
a botched Pavlova
trust issues

off-ramp roses
a night on the lam
second thoughts

a butterfly
an admission
three lies

floss
coffee ice cream
a hole in one

the Kama Sutra
an interior decorator
a remorse-filled sigh

a Tic Tac
a ballerina's ankle
enough rope

my foot
your bad
an epiphany—

I'd almost forgotten

your cock
your cock
your cock

THE DRACAENA PLANT IN MY APARTMENT ON BEACHWOOD DR.

1.
when I see I've overwatered it again, I jab
the turkey baster into the rust-colored runoff
before the water spills over
onto the hardwood floor.

in our mid-town apartment,
the harsh light sears the spiky leaves.

it reminds me of summer,
when you left me here on Beachwood Dr.
and I shot Demerol
my rust-colored blood backing up in the syringe,
the same pierce of yellow light,
the sharp spike breaking my skin.

2.
I remember what you said about overkill,
how I could love a thing to death.

my jaundiced face mirrored
the ailing yellow of the dracaena's tired leaves,
the green of it, peaked, off-color.
my sad visage the hue of drowning,
the flood of the Demerol too much like
pleasure.

3.
the dracaena hides a stain
on the hardwood floor in the
shape of a man. A murky, splayed patch
between the closet and the bed.

since you disappeared, some nights
I lie down on that stain,
my body mimicking the way I'd lie
on top of you, arms and legs akimbo.
I imagine you, oozing out
onto the hardwood, a mess.

4.
the landlord, under duress, admitted
that a dead man *had* lain there
till long past rigor, seeping fluids
like an overwatered plant
till he and the floor had organically
merged into one.

THE LOVERS ON PFEIFFER BEACH

I don't think you saw them.
Scant feet above us, sheltered
in a hollow below the cliffs.

Like watching a porno film, the way she sucked
her surfer's lovely cock, her lush blondness
shimmering as she dipped her head, his hard body
illuminated in the harsh morning sun.

We were sitting on a blanket, sucking
Stoli straight from the bottle.
I pointed them out on the cliff, but you were busy
with your phone. "No service," you groused.
You were always somewhere else.

I watched over your shoulder as he turned
her, to enter from behind, his big hands cupping
her breasts, his tireless ass thrusting, thrusting.

Jagger's "(I Can't Get No) Satisfaction" kept playing in my head
like our theme song; the one you couldn't hear.
When I pocketed your phone, you asked me to
marry you, again.

On the cliff, the lovers shuddered, broke apart, then embraced,
their blonde congruency so at odds with our mis-matched desires.

Above us, kamikaze seagulls circled. They threw their heads back and
screeched. You reached for me, but
I was not yet drunk enough. I would never
be drunk enough.

On the cliff, the blond pressed her naked breasts against her lover's chest.
He stared over her shoulder at me, his eyes a dare.
Then he put his hand to his lips
and blew a kiss. I caught it in my mouth.
I handed you the phone and started down the beach
with the bottle of Stoli,

his sweet kiss languishing on my tongue.

SNAPSHOTS AND LIES

1.
our bodies are a haven from August.

this summer all we do is rut

mattress on the carpet
him on me

a miasma of scorching discontent.

2.
dingy sheets.
the dryer eats them and my future

gets stuck in the holes.

3.
how did I know he wanted that baby?

4.
at the window,
he smokes Marlboros, taps ashes
on the losers below.

5.
there's not enough air to go around.

6.
I found a corpse in the kitchen, I tell him.

7.
he flicks his dead daddy's Zippo
again and again,

surveys the neon-tinged city.

8.
I want to steal something important.

9.
I reach for his pride on the window ledge.
he flicks me away like a gnat.

10.
the tv's been broken since May.

KEEP WALKING
(ON LAS PALMAS AVE., APPROACHING
HOLLYWOOD BLVD., I HEAR A SCREAM)

In the spill of the porch lamp the girl looks fourteen,
cowering in the courtyard of this windy night,
cheap stilettos stemming her pale legs up into tiny shorts.

Two men the size of refrigerators
slap her face like she's meat that needs
tenderizing. One stands behind her, pins her arms;
the other brute yells in her face:
"You will fuck who I say, when I say!"
When he pulls back to smack her again I look away.

In Hollywood the streets talk trash, hold murder
in their asphalt, blood in the potholes,
used hypodermics float in the gutters, rats
dance on the lawns.

The girl lurches, stumbles in those 5-inch heels,
the only thing separating her from the ground.

The two men toss her back and forth
like a football. Her eyes catch mine.
When her pimp sees me he hollers in my face.
"Keep walking!"

I'm late. My dealer is impatient.
I do what I'm told.

High on pot. Tequila. Fear.
I head into the neon of Hollywood Blvd.,
keep walking till I can't hear her screams.

WHY I PREFER INJECTABLE NARCOTICS

(the truth that impales me each time i get straight)

it's all cake once i've found a good vein.
i surrender to the dazzling foreplay
loosen the belt, ease back the plunger
watch my blood flood the syringe.
the gasp, the breath-catch just before i jam
the plunger down, just like
you plunge into me *(my cheeks flush)*
and the rush? the ride? the afterglow?
better than sex. correction:
better than sex with you *(i mean)*.

FOLIE À TROIS

1.
I call my best friend Vicki;
she answers with sex in her throat.
Your husband is busy.
He can't come to the phone.

2.
They've been fucking since I was cast
in a Brecht play at the Hyperion Theatre
in Silverlake.

And they weren't.

3.
I play Prostitute #1.
I speak my lines in Vicki's voice.

Brecht says *people remain what they are*
even if their faces fall apart.

4.
After my 3-week anniversary 'gift,'
(her straw blond hairs on my pillow)
nothing surprises me.

5.
Ronnie may be having second thoughts;
he says marriage to a junkie is not
what it's cracked up to be.

6.
I am addicted to bad men, sex, and
opiates. I wrongly thought my husband was
addicted to me.

7.
And Vicki, addicted only to breaking up
someone else's marriage, tells herself
Ronnie deserves better, plans a white wedding,
refines the guest list in her head.

CRIME SCENE OF LOVE

I watched her nose flatten against my fist.
Her blood splattered the bone white walls like a Pollock,

cast off ruining the cream-colored sofa,
jealousy stippling my dress.

Outside the telephone wires were electric with
my indiscretions,

our latest bout choreographed as Blunt Force Trauma,
a Balanchine pas de deux.

Vicki crumpled backward into the half-light
of late afternoon.

When she spoke her lines they came out
not as a growl exactly, more a victorious ululation;

her high-pitched wail like a she-wolf in heat.

I saw the blood on her less-
than-perfect teeth.

QUIET CANDY

After you kicked me out,
and moved Vicki in,
I spilled my guts to the Armenian drug dealer
at the Glendale Galleria.

He told me he'd fix
my Porsche, pay off my credit cards, keep me
in cashmere and coke,
if I'd let him.
He'd dress me in silk that grazed my ass,
said he liked the whiteness
of my thighs, said if I were his, he'd keep me
out of the sun.

There I was, strung out on dope,
all lanky, pale-skinned
need.

The Armenian drug dealer bought me
4-inch Louboutins and a leash,
bought me
a Stetson to shade my face.
I let him move me
into his condo in Glendale.

The Armenian drug dealer liked to drive
the freeways, had business
in San Diego and Oceanside
and San Juan Capistrano, liked the top down
on the Beamer, liked the way my hair whipped
in the wind. He liked fucking me
in his 3-car garage, pinned
against the hood. He could do it for hours
when I'd let him.

The Armenian drug dealer liked candy on his arm,
quiet candy
that was loud in the bedroom. He liked my ass
raised on a pillow, legs spread
like a Gullwing Mercedes.

I let him do anything he wanted.
He wanted me to tell him about you.

I told the Armenian drug dealer
how you wrapped Vicki in my mother's embroidered shawl,
how you gave her my grandmother's amethyst ring.
How you used a rifle to make your point.
How you could only come if you tied me up.
How you papered our bedroom with lies.

The Armenian drug dealer wanted to storm your house
wanted to tie you up with the same ropes you used on me
wanted to rip my mother's shawl from Vicki's shoulders
wanted to take the rifle out of your hands
wanted to bring back my grandmother's amethyst ring.

So I let him.

COERCION

after a poem by Margaret Atwood

Nobody held him down, twisted
his arm, shoved in a needle.

Back then, we fit together like
cooking spoons in a drawer.

Bent spoons. A cadaver drawer.

DIVORCE COURT BARBIE™ (KEN™ DRIVES AWAY WITH ALL MY THINGS)

I was no Fairytale Bride™
but I came with a Barbie Daybed,™ A Bath Fun Playset,™
and a large, pink Desire Barbie Dildo Vibrator™
for when Ken™ forgot to come home.

But he couldn't keep it in his Ken Fashionistas Trousers.™
He parked his Glam Convertible w/ Silver Rims™
in Skipper's™ driveway,
stashed his GPS in her Long & Short of It Pants.™

Then he drove out of her Dinner Date Playset™
and back to our Barbie Dream House,™
packed a few things in my Store-It-All Carrying Case™
and dropped me at the Barbie Grand Hotel™
like I was so much Euro-trash.

Look, Your Honor, nobody came with a warranty,
but unlike Ken,™ my intentions were pure;
I lived up to my Good Housekeeping Seal.

The Ken & Barbie Have Sex Before Marriage Playset™
made sure Ken knew what he was getting into.
Then he got into Skipper.™

I know what you must think, Your Honor.
There are names for dolls like me:

Bad Luck Barbie™
Throwaway Barbie™
The one Ken™ swears he wouldn't love
if I were the Last Girl On Earth Barbie.™

The one who's rendered worthless once you trash the box.

CHANCE ENCOUNTER

Tooling down Sunset, I saw them, her riding shotgun in the blue, beater Chevy, him at the wheel. They were one lane over, two cars up. I pulled parallel, rolled down my window, stuck out my arm, and waved. Vicki slumped in shame the way she had when I'd broken her nose. Her face turning white as the bandages she was still wearing, I watched her slink in the seat until she disappeared, revealing my husband, red-faced, apoplectic. "Why can't you just leave us alone?" he yelled.

Like I was stalking them. Like I even cared.

WHY I ALMOST FORGAVE YOU
(PERCHÉ TI HO QUASI PERDONATO)

Because your eyes were blue as Curaçao
and your table manners, impeccable

Because inside your head I was smooth
as Michelangelo's *Aurora*

Because the night was in cahoots with the street lamps
and *La Dolce Vita* was an amusement ride

Because the light was saffron yellow in October
and the purple irises were not in bloom

Because I was drunk on vodka sauce
Because I was drunk on you

Because the gnocchi at Dan Tana's were to die for
Because you swore to die
before you'd lie to me

But I sucked you off
under the table anyway

And the moon hid behind my skirt
and we shared cannoli for dessert

And you didn't know:

ricotta sat cool on my tongue
and the Campari tasted as bitter as love

KILLING RONNIE'S BABY

My body is a time bomb.
Invaded. Knocked up.

I think Conquered.
I think Tethered.
I think Run!
I think Bad Dad.
I think Narcissist.
I think Divorce.
I think Single Mom.
I think Slow Death.

I don't think.
I make the appointment.

ONCE MORE, RONNIE SAID, FOR OLD TIME'S SAKE.

In our bedroom in Silverlake he ties my wrists
to the bedposts one last time, checks
the knots.

Positioning his body on top of mine, he
slips into me, cock growing like a cancer
inside. *Move, dammit!* he barks.

Then he licks my face, dog spittle
pooling in my neck's hollow,
raspy tongue a reek of toothpaste and pot.
I stare past his dirty blondness at a
framed Schiele print on the wall—
a rapacious threesome (man and two
women, going at it like rabbits).
It could be us.

I want to pick up the phone, invite Vicki
to join us. Maybe she could take over?
It's troubling, the joy I feel at the thought,
now I'm the odd one out; now
my husband isn't mine.

Don't move, dammit! When he comes
he wants me rigid—
a depository—
like I'm there but not there.

I shoot junk in my veins like Ronnie
shoots into me. Without thinking. It's
suddenly clear.

I can see my future
and if I don't stop,
I'm not in it.

APPEARANCES

Mother said a lady is always clean, well-dressed,
and presentable, even when dying inside.

Dr. Tim looked me up and down
with undisguised
approval.

I'd finally washed
my hair, and it hung
in loose waves down my back.

I'd put on the size 0 mini-dress
with lace sleeves
(to show off my legs
and hide the needletracks).

Sliding my feet into a pair of high
heels felt right
for the first time in ages.

I'd slipped my wedding ring on-
to a chain, clipped it
around my neck.

I'd drunk black
coffee, forced down an apple,
then thrown it up in the sink,

put a coat on and looked
less anorexic.

In the waiting room
I'd read *Vogue's*
Fall issue, cover to cover.

Today I was as beautiful
as any model.

Dr. Tim checked me up and down.
With my new look,
the shrink hardly knew me.

I fingered the razor blade in my pocket.

"You look like a million bucks."

ABOUT THE AUTHOR

Alexis Rhone Fancher is the author of *How I Lost My Virginity To Michael Cohen and other heart stab poems,* (2014), *State of Grace: The Joshua Elegies,* (2015), and *Enter Here (2017).* She is published in *Best American Poetry 2016, Rattle, Hobart, Slipstream, Plume, Nashville Review, Diode, Glass, Tinderbox, Verse Daily,* and elsewhere. Her photos are published world wide, including *River Styx,* and the covers of *Witness, Heyday, The Chiron Review,* and *Nerve Cowboy.* A multiple Pushcart Prize and Best of the Net nominee, Alexis is poetry editor of *Cultural Weekly.* She lives in Los Angeles. Visit: www.alexisrhonefancher.com

ACKNOWLEDGEMENTS

Grateful acknowledgement to the editors of the following publications in which these poems have previously appeared:

Fjords Review: "Things I Put in My Mouth"
great weather for MEDIA: "Once more," Ronnie said, "for old time's sake."
Plume: "Quiet Candy"
Public Pool: "Why I Prefer Injectable Narcotics," & "Why I Almost Forgave You *(Perché ti ho quasi perdonato)*"
Rattle: "The Dracaena Plant in My Apartment on Beachwood Dr."
Red Flag Poetry: "Coercion"
Rust + Moth: "Folie à Trois"
Tinderbox Poetry Journal: "Appearances"
Toad: "The Lovers on Pfeiffer Beach"; "Keep Walking"
Vox Populi: "Divorce Court Barbie™ (Ken™ Drives Away with All of My Things)"
Wherewithal: "Snapshots and Lies"

"Snapshots and Lies" was a finalist for the *Wherewithal* Poetry Contest, 2015

I am hugely indebted to Michelle Bitting, Chanel Brenner, and Tresha Haefner-Rubinstein for their encouragement, editorial prowess, and friendship during the writing of this chapbook.

PATRONS

Moon Tide Press would like to thank the following people for their support in helping publish the finest poetry from the Southern California region. To sign up as a patron, visit www.moontidepress.com or send an email to publisher@moontidepress.com.

Anonymous
Robin Axworthy
Conner Brenner
Bill Cushing
Susan Davis
Peggy Dobreer
Dennis Gowans
Half Off Books
Jim & Vicky Hoggatt
Ron Koertge & Bianca Richards
Ray & Christi Lacoste
Zachary & Tammy Locklin
Lincoln McElwee
David McIntire
José Enrique Medina
Michael Miller & Rachanee Srisavasdi
Terri Niccum
Ronny & Richard Morago
Jennifer Smith
Andrew Turner
Mariano Zaro

ALSO AVAILABLE FROM MOON TIDE PRESS

The Moon, My Lover, My Mother, & the Dog, Daniel McGinn (2018)
Lullaby of Teeth: An Anthology of Southern California Poetry (2017)
Angels in Seven, Michael Miller (2016)
A Likely Story, Robbi Nester (2014)
Embers on the Stairs, Ruth Bavetta (2014)
The Green of Sunset, John Brantingham (2013)
The Savagery of Bone, Timothy Matthew Perez (2013)
The Silence of Doorways, Sharon Venezio (2013)
Cosmos: An Anthology of Southern California Poetry (2012)
Straws and Shadows, Irena Praitis (2012)
In the Lake of Your Bones, Peggy Dobreer (2012)
I Was Building Up to Something, Susan Davis (2011)
Hopeless Cases, Michael Kramer (2011)
One World, Gail Newman (2011)
What We Ache For, Eric Morago (2010)
Now and Then, Lee Mallory (2009)
Pop Art: An Anthology of Southern California Poetry (2010)
In the Heaven of Never Before, Carine Topal (2008)
A Wild Region, Kate Buckley (2008)
Carving in Bone: An Anthology of Orange County Poetry (2007)
Kindness from a Dark God, Ben Trigg (2007)
A Thin Strands of Lights, Ricki Mandeville (2006)
Sleepyhead Assassins, Mindy Nettifee (2006)
Tide Pools: An Anthology of Orange County Poetry (2006)
Lost American Nights: Lyrics & Poems, Michael Ubaldini (2006)

CPSIA information can be obtained
at www.ICGtesting.com
Printed in the USA
BVHW030449200123
656708BV00013B/45